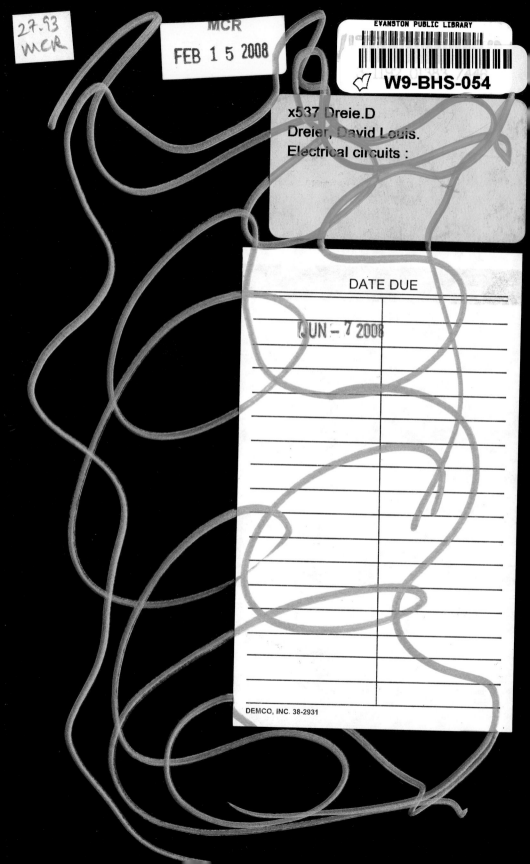

DATE DUE

EXPLORING SCIENCE

ELECTRICAL CIRCUITS

HARNESSING ELECTRICITY

BY DAVID DREIER

Content Adviser: William Hudson, Ph.D., Electrical and Computer
Engineering & Technology Chair, Minnesota State University, Mankato

Science Adviser: Terrence E. Young Jr., M.Ed., M.L.S.,
Jefferson Parish (Louisiana) Public School System

Reading Adviser: Rosemary G. Palmer, Ph.D., Department of Literacy,
College of Education, Boise State University

Compass Point Books • Minneapolis, Minnesota

Compass Point Books • 3109 West 50th Street, #115 • Minneapolis, MN 55410

Visit Compass Point Books on the Internet at *www.compasspointbooks.com*
or e-mail your request to *custserv@compasspointbooks.com*

Photographs ©: Lori Bye/Compass Point Books, Cover; Ullstein-Hechtenberg/Peter Arnold, Inc., 4; Mark Garlick/
Photo Researchers, Inc., 5; Mark Burnett / Photo Researchers, Inc., 8; Ray Pfortner / Peter Arnold, Inc., 9; Weath-
erstock/Peter Arnold, Inc., 10; Shutterstock/Thomas Mounsey, 12; Shutterstock/Povl E. Petersen, 13; Shutter-
stock/Randy McKown, 14; Shutterstock/Merlin, 17; Shutterstock/Adam Majchrzak, 18; Shutterstock/Ilya Rabkin,
21; Library of Congress, 22; Bettmann/CORBIS, 23; Shutterstock/Chepe Nicoli, 24; Gusto/Photo Researchers,
Inc., 25; Leonard Lessin/Peter Arnold, Inc., 28; Nelson Morris/Photo Researchers, Inc, 29; Shutterstock/Scott
Rothstein, 30; D. Arky/Photex/zefa/Corbis, 31; ullstein-Oed/Peter Arnold, Inc., 32; MARTIN BOND/Peter
Arnold, Inc., 33; Peter Frischmuth / Peter Arnold, Inc., 35; Peter Turnley/Corbis, 36; Shutterstock/Ingvald
Kaldhussater, 38; Dr. John Brackenbury / Photo Researchers, Inc., 40; Adrianna Williams/zefa/Corbis, 42;
Shutterstock/Alexander Remy Levine, 43; Roger Ressmeyer/Corbis, 44; NORBERT WU/Minden Pictures, 46.

Editor: Anthony Wacholtz
Designer: The Design Lab
Page Production: Lori Bye
Photo Researcher: Lori Bye
Illustrator: Ashlee Schultz

Art Director: Jaime Martens
Creative Director: Keith Griffin
Editorial Director: Nick Healy
Managing Editor: Catherine Neitge

Library of Congress Cataloging-in-Publication Data
Dreier, David Louis.
 Electrical circuits : harnessing electricity/by David Dreier; illustrator Ashlee Schultz.
  p. cm.—(Exploring science)
 ISBN-13: 978-0-7565-3267-3 (library binding)
 ISBN-10: 0-7565-3267-1 (library binding)
 1. Electric circuits—Juvenile literature.
 2. Electricity—Juvenile literature. I. Schultz, Ashlee. II. Title.

 TK148.D73 2007
 537—dc22   2007004603

About the Author

David L. Dreier is a science writer and editor. He studied journalism
and science writing at Northwestern University in Evanston, Illinois.
After college, he worked for several years as a science and medical
writer at several publications. Later he was on the staff of Science
Year, the science and technology annual of World Book Encyclopedia.
He was managing editor of Science Year for six years. He has been
a freelance writer and editor since 2003.

TABLE OF CONTENTS

CHAPTER ONE

What Is Electricity?

OUR MODERN WORLD runs on electricity. Huge power plants generate electricity and send it out on long transmission lines. In homes, offices, and factories, electricity moves through circuits to light houses and run machinery. We use electricity day and night without giving it much thought. If we flip a wall switch, a light begins to shine. If we press the power button on a television, the screen comes to life. Electricity is available when we need it.

Power plants provide much of the electricity we use every day.

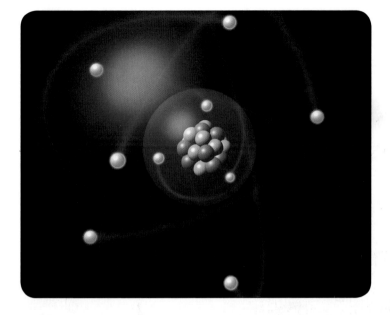

ATOMS AND ELECTRIC CHARGE

Electricity is a force of nature. It comes from a property called electric charge that is on particles within atoms—the smallest units of matter. An atom contains three kinds of particles: protons, neutrons, and electrons. Protons and neutrons make up the nucleus, or center, of an atom. Protons have a positive electric charge, and neutrons have no charge. Electrons whirl around the nucleus with a negative charge. Protons are heavier than electrons, but an electron's negative charge has the same strength as a proton's positive charge, keeping the atom's charge neutral.

The nucleus of an atom is made up of protons (blue) and neutrons (turquoise). Electrons (pink) swarm around the nucleus.

Most atoms have electrons that circle the nucleus at two or more levels, called electron shells, from the nucleus. The oxygen atom, for example, has two shells. The inner shell holds two electrons—the most the inner shell of any atom can hold—and the outer shell contains six electrons. The biggest atoms have up to seven electron shells.

Although an atom has no charge, it is possible for an atom to gain or lose electrons. It then acquires a charge and is called an ion. An atom that loses one or more electrons acquires a positive charge and is called a cation. An atom that gains one or more electrons becomes negatively charged and is called an anion.

LIKE CHARGES REPEL, UNLIKE CHARGES ATTRACT

Charges that are the same repel each other, and opposite charges attract each other. Therefore, two electrons (or two protons) will repel each other, but an electron and a proton are drawn together. Cations and anions behave in the same way.

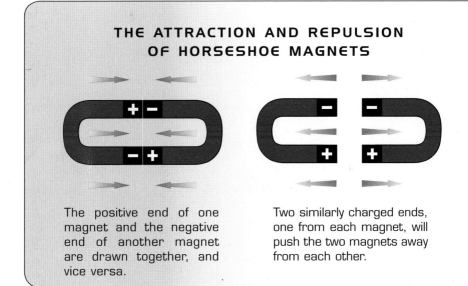

THE ATTRACTION AND REPULSION OF HORSESHOE MAGNETS

The positive end of one magnet and the negative end of another magnet are drawn together, and vice versa.

Two similarly charged ends, one from each magnet, will push the two magnets away from each other.

The attraction of opposite charges can be seen with static electricity. With static electricity, positive and negative charges have been separated and are trying to recombine to form electrically neutral atoms.

You can experience static electricity trying to become neutral by scuffing your shoes along a carpeted surface. When you put your finger near a metal object, a spark will jump from your finger to the metal. You picked up a negative charge by breaking electrons free from the carpet. When you put your finger near the metal, your negative charge pushed electrons in the metal atoms away, causing the atoms in the metal to

become positive ions. The extra electrons in your body then jumped from your finger to the metal.

Lightning works much the same way. It is a giant spark caused by a buildup of charges in clouds that are trying to become neutral.

ELECTRICITY AND MAGNETISM

Electricity is also closely related to magnetism. Together they form a fundamental force of the universe called the electromagnetic force. In fact, through the use of electromagnets,

An electrostatic generator, a device that produces a large buildup of static electricity, can cause individual hairs to repel each other because they are similarly charged.

electricity can be used to produce magnetism. Electromagnets are magnets that contain a coil of wire wrapped around an iron core. When an electric current flows through the wire, it causes groups of atoms in the core to line up. The alignment of these atoms produces a strong magnetic field.

Even more important, magnetism can produce electricity. Researchers in the 1800s learned that an electric current is created when a coil of metal wire is moved through a magnetic field. The magnetic field interacts with the electrons in the

Large electromagnets used in junkyards can pick up scrap metal and even entire automobiles.

Nature's Fireworks

Lightning is one of the most dramatic spectacles in nature. It results from an enormous buildup of static electricity in a storm cloud. Scientists think this buildup occurs when soft, icy particles called graupel collide with smaller ice particles in a cloud, taking electrons from them. The graupel, now with a negative charge, fall to the lower part of the cloud. At the same time, the particles that lost their electrons become positively charged and are carried by winds to the upper parts of the cloud. In this way, the cloud develops two areas of separated, opposite electric charges.

Most lightning either occurs within a cloud or goes from one cloud to another. The separated areas of electric charges in the clouds flow together in a flash of lightning to recreate neutral atoms.

Many lightning bolts strike the earth as well. This form of lightning is called cloud-to-ground (CG) lightning.

Most lightning results from a buildup of opposite electric charges within clouds.

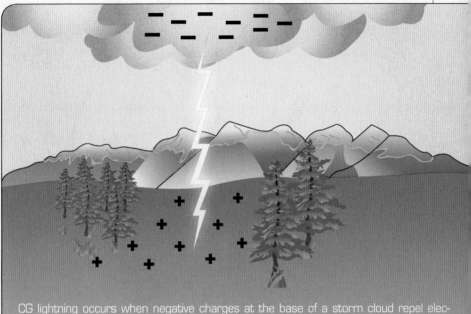

CG lightning occurs when negative charges at the base of a storm cloud repel electrons in the ground. The ground area under the cloud becomes positively charged. When the positive charge on the ground and the negative charge at the base of the cloud build up, they are powerfully attracted. The electrons in the cloud then stream toward the ground in a channel about the width of a pencil. The surging electrons release energy that lights up the channel, creating a bright, zigzagging flash.

The energy released by the bolt heats the air in the channel to about 54,000 degrees Fahrenheit (30,000 degrees Celsius)—making the air five times as hot as the surface of the sun. The heat causes the channel carrying the electrons to the ground to expand violently and produce a shock wave that we hear as thunder.

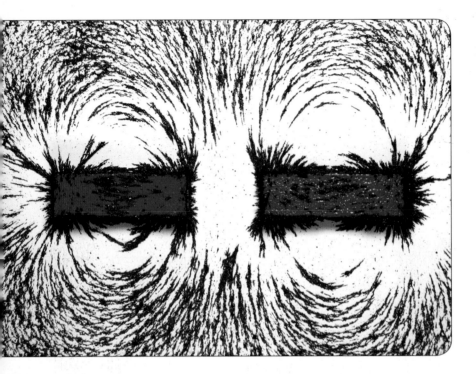

wire and causes them to move. The same effect is produced if a magnet is moved through a coil of wire. In either case, the wire or the magnet is moving, causing electrons in the wire to flow.

The generation of an electric current with a magnetic field is called electromagnetic induction. The discovery of electromagnetic induction eventually led to the ability to generate electricity on a large scale, allowing us to power our modern, electrified world.

Iron filings placed near two bar magnets will align along the magnetic field lines.

Electric Currents

SOME PEOPLE HAVE wondered whether light-
ning could be harnessed for useful purposes, but no one has
found a way to do it. To benefit us in our everyday lives, electric
charges must flow in an orderly way. This flow is known as a
current. Electric current is measured in amperes, or amps. Both
positive and negative charges can flow as a current, but the
current in the electrical wires that bring power to our homes
and workplaces is composed of negatively charged electrons.

One amp is approximately the current in a small flashlight.

CONDUCTORS AND INSULATORS

To carry a current, a material must be a conductor, meaning electricity can easily flow through the material. Metals are the most common conductors. Silver is a very good metallic con-

ductor, but copper is almost as good. Because copper is much cheaper than silver, most wires are made of copper.

Scientists say materials like copper and silver are good conductors because they have low resistance to electric current. Resistance is a force that opposes the flow of charges. Some materials—known as insulators—have a high resistance to electric currents.

The resistance of a conductor can vary. Imagine what happens when water flows through pipes. A wide pipe allows more water through than a thin pipe, and therefore has less resistance. In the same respect, a

Most electrical wires are surrounded by rubber or plastic coverings. These two materials are excellent insulators and protect people from electric shocks.

> **DID YOU KNOW?**
>
> When some materials are cooled to extremely low tempera-
> tures, they lose all resistance to an electric current. These
> materials are then called superconductors.

thin copper wire has much higher resistance to a current than a thick copper wire. Since a bigger wire has more area for the electrons to flow through, the resistance is lower than for a thinner wire of the same metal.

Resistance to a current generates heat, which can be useful. For example, the resistance of a lightbulb's filament, or thread-like conductor, causes the filament to heat up and glow brightly. Electric stoves and electric heaters also use this effect.

HOW CONDUCTORS WORK

A conductor contains atoms with loosely attached electrons. For example, both copper and silver have a single electron in their outer shell. These electrons are held by the atom with such a weak bond that they can break away with ease. In contrast, the outer electrons of an insulator are tightly bound to the atom.

The atoms of a conductor are constantly losing and gaining electrons as the electrons jump from one atom to another.

Even when a wire is not carrying a current, it is still full of electric charges—they are just going in random directions. The electrons are like a crowd of people in a tunnel walking every which way and bumping into each another. But when the wire carries a current, it's like a tunnel full of people who are all headed the same way.

GIVING ELECTRIC CHARGES A PUSH

But what makes the electric charges move together? Voltage—a kind of "electric pressure"—pushes the electric charges

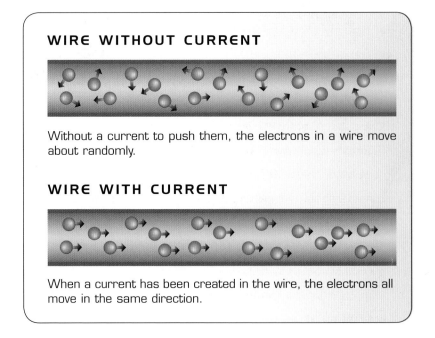

WIRE WITHOUT CURRENT

Without a current to push them, the electrons in a wire move about randomly.

WIRE WITH CURRENT

When a current has been created in the wire, the electrons all move in the same direction.

so that they flow in the same direction. Without voltage, no electrons would flow in a wire.

Voltage is the difference in potential energy, or stored energy, between two points. A boulder that has been pushed to the top of a hill contains a lot of potential energy. In fact, it would equal the amount of energy that was required to push it up to that high place. If the boulder rolled back down the hill, that potential energy would be converted to kinetic energy, the energy of motion.

Many energy conversions occur during a roller coaster ride. The potential energy peaks as the cars reach the top of the loop, but that energy becomes kinetic energy as the cars hurtle downward.

Voltage is measured in units called volts. Various voltages are used for electric currents. Some flashlight batteries, for example, have a voltage of just 1.5 volts. That means that one terminal, or end, of the battery has a potential energy 1.5 volts higher than the other end (which has 0.0 volts). One terminal of the battery, called the anode (the flat, bottom end), has an excess of electrons, making it negatively charged. The other terminal, the cathode (the end with a bump), has a shortage of electrons and is positively charged. It is this imbalance of electric charges that creates the voltage difference.

The number and type of batteries a device needs depends on the voltage required. A basic television remote control uses two AA batteries, but many remote-control toy cars use four AA batteries.

HOW DO BATTERIES WORK?

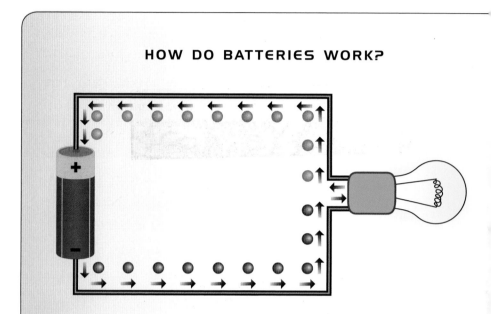

Electrons flow from the negative end of the battery to the positive end of the battery. Their movement gives them kinetic energy. On their way, they give up most of that energy to the filament of the lightbulb, which causes the bulb to light. Electrons will continue to flow until the anode can no longer give up electrons or the cathode can no longer accept them. The battery then needs to be replaced.

TWO KINDS OF ELECTRIC CURRENT

The electric current from a battery is called direct current, or DC. With a DC current, electric charges always move in the same direction. Electrons only move forward at a rate of about 2 inches (5 centimeters) a minute. But there are so many atoms in a wire that more than a million trillion electrons pass any point in the wire every second. The electric charges flowing in a wire also create an invisible electric field around the wire. Energy is transmitted through the electric field almost instantly.

Imagine a tube full of marbles. If you give the marble on one end a push, all the other marbles will move at the same instant. You have transmitted energy all the way down the line of marbles, even though each marble has moved just a small distance. DC current works much the same way, but it is the difference in voltage between two points that provides the push to set the energy in motion.

Electricity that comes into our homes and offices from power plants is called alternating current, or AC. With an AC current, the electrons in a wire do not move constantly forward as they do in a DC current. Instead, they stay in one place and vibrate back and forth many times a second.

To understand how AC current works, picture a bicycle wheel mounted horizontally on a rod. You stand on one side of the wheel, and a friend stands on the opposite side. Your friend places the palm of one hand against the tire while you move the wheel back and forth rapidly. Your friend's hand will quickly get warm from the friction caused by the movement of the tire. You have transmitted energy through the wheel to

your friend's hand. The back-and-forth motion of electrons in a wire is similar to the back-and-forth motion of the wheel.

If electrons move slowly, or just move back and forth, what happens when you switch on a flashlight or a table lamp? Why does it turn on instantly? Even though electric charges move slowly or only vibrate, the energy produced moves extremely fast.

The vibrating motion of a guitar string is similar to the movement of electrons in an AC current.

How AC Beat DC

The widespread use of electricity began in the late 1800s. In 1882, Thomas A. Edison established an electricity-generating system in New York City. His Pearl Street electrical power station provided electricity for lighting part of the city.

Edison's system used DC current, but the DC system had limitations. For one thing, the current could not be transmitted very far. Therefore, lighting a city the size of New York would require hundreds of power stations. Also, DC was not able to power many kinds of factory motors. The current provided by the Edison Company had a voltage of 110 volts and could not be changed. Some motors, however, required other voltages.

A wealthy inventor and businessman named George Westinghouse decided to compete with Edison. He bought the rights to an AC system invented by an electrical engineer, Nikola Tesla. Tesla's system made it possible to transmit electricity to a whole city from a few power stations. Devices called transformers could be used to increase or decrease the voltage

Besides constructing the Pearl Street electricity-generating system, Thomas Edison (1847–1931) is credited with more than 1,000 inventions, including a reliable lightbulb and the phonograph.

at the power station. At a higher voltage, the current could be sent over a long distance with fewer losses. Other transformers at distant locations could then reduce the voltage back to the required level for lighting or motors.

The superiority of AC current was soon obvious to everyone except Edison. He tried to convince people that his system was the best, but by the end of the 1800s, all new electricity-generating plants supplied AC power.

Nikola Tesla (1856–1943) generated artificial lightning in his laboratory.

Electrical Circuits

IMAGINE A RAILROAD track with no beginning or end. A train moves endlessly around the circular track. The train keeps moving as long as the entire track is in place. But if a section of track is removed, the train comes to a stop.

An electric current is like that train. For a current to move, it needs a path called a circuit. When a current is turned on, a field of electricity forms instantly around the entire circuit, and all the electric charges within it begin to move. If the circuit is broken at any point, the electric current stops.

Like a model train moving around a toy railroad track, current flows continuously through a circuit.

An electrical circuit has three basic parts: an energy source, an output device, and wires or cables. An energy source can be a battery or an electrical generator. An output device is anything that puts the current to good use, such as a lamp, an electric motor, or a radio. The wires or cables transmit the electric current.

A circuit usually contains a switch to turn the current on and off. Turning off the switch creates a gap in the circuit that stops the flow of charges until the current is needed again. A circuit in which the current has been stopped is called an open

In a hair dryer, electricity travels up the cord from an outlet. The electricity powers the fan (blue), which blows air over the heated filament (orange). Switches (brown) control the speed of the fan.

circuit. When the switch is closed to eliminate the gap so electricity can flow, the circuit is called a closed circuit.

TYPES OF CIRCUITS

There are two main kinds of circuits: series and parallel. A series circuit contains one path for the current to follow. If there is more than one output device in the circuit, they are connected in a series, or line. If one of these output devices fails, the circuit is broken and the current stops.

This type of circuit is used mostly in simple equipment that has only one output device, such as a flashlight. One advantage of series wiring is that it enables voltages to be added. For example, a flashlight that requires 3 volts uses two 1.5-volt batteries.

Series circuits have sometimes caused problems for people. Years ago, for example, strands of Christmas tree bulbs were wired in series. Every time a bulb blew out, the entire string of bulbs went dark. It was then necessary to test every bulb in the string to find the one that had failed.

A parallel circuit avoids that problem. Output devices in a parallel circuit are connected with two or more wires running in parallel, or side by side. Current runs through all the wires. With this arrangement, if one output device fails, the others keep getting current and stay on.

TYPES OF CIRCUITS

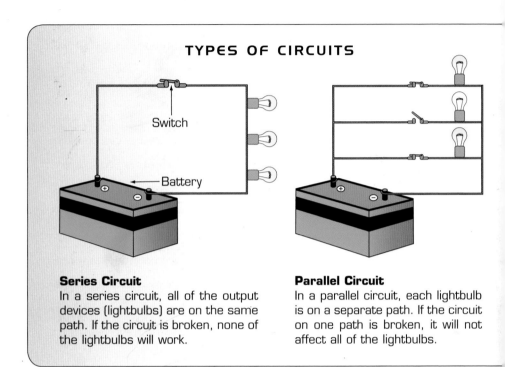

Series Circuit
In a series circuit, all of the output devices (lightbulbs) are on the same path. If the circuit is broken, none of the lightbulbs will work.

Parallel Circuit
In a parallel circuit, each lightbulb is on a separate path. If the circuit on one path is broken, it will not affect all of the lightbulbs.

All the AC wiring in a home is parallel. This form of wiring makes it possible to turn off an appliance but use a lamp or other device that is on the same circuit. If series wiring were used in homes, all the devices on a particular circuit would have to be turned on for any of them to operate.

Parallel wiring allows all the devices on a circuit to operate at the same voltage. The voltage does not change if an appliance or other device is added to the circuit. Only devices that operate at the same voltage can be connected in parallel.

The Smallest Circuits in the World

The first general-purpose computer, known as **ENIAC**, was built in 1946. It took up an entire room and weighed more than 30 tons (27 metric tons)! ENIAC had to be big because it used vacuum tubes. Also used in early television sets, vacuum tubes were bulky and burned out frequently. Still, despite ENIAC's large size and weight, it could do far less than a modern computer.

The invention of the transistor in 1947 changed everything. Transistors were much smaller and more dependable than vacuum tubes. By the late 1950s, transistors were replacing vacuum tubes in televisions, computers, and other kinds of electronic equipment. They had two basic functions: to turn electricity in a circuit on and off and to strengthen the current when necessary.

But even with transistors, computers were large, and the circuits had to be assembled by hand. This was a time-consuming task since computer circuits had an enormous number of components.

Then, in 1958, a researcher in Texas named Jack Kilby invented the integrated circuit. The first step in building an integrated circuit is to draw a large, detailed design

Because transistors (left) are much smaller than vacuum tubes, electronics using transistors could be built in a much smaller size.

of the circuit. The design is photographed, and the image is reduced to about the size of a fingernail. This reduced-size image is called a mask. High-energy light is used to imprint hundreds of copies of the mask onto a thin wafer of silicon, which is a conductor and an insulator. Unneeded portions of the circuit are then removed, and a metal conductor is added to form electrical connections. Finally, the silicon wafer is cut apart into individual "chips," each containing the entire circuit. Kilby's invention made it possible to make computers smaller and cheaper.

The development of integrated circuits has progressed greatly since 1958. Today's integrated circuits contain hundreds of millions of components. The transistors on a chip are so small that hundreds could fit inside a red blood cell.

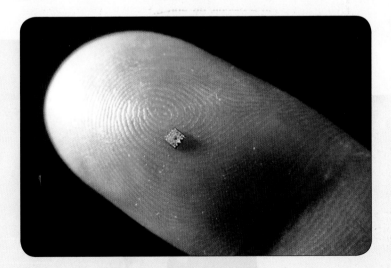

Integrated circuits have been built increasingly smaller since 1958.

ELECTRIC SWITCHES

Many kinds of switches are used to control electric currents, but every switch has the same purpose: to open or close a circuit. A switch contains two metal points, called contacts. The switch can push the contacts together or pull them apart. When the switch is turned on, the contacts are brought together to complete the circuit. Electricity can then flow in the circuit. When the switch is turned off, the connection between the contacts is broken, and the current stops.

A switch that does not make a connection between the two metal contacts breaks the flow of electricity, resulting in an open circuit.

The most common switches in our homes are the ones on walls that turn room lights on and off. These are called toggle switches because they move back and forth. Other common kinds of switches include push-buttons and knobs that are turned in a clockwise direction. These types of switches are found on many lamps.

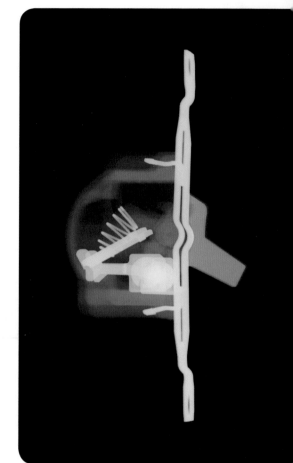

Whatever their type, switches are always made to insulate the current they control. The insulation protects users from getting an electric shock. On most switches, the part that we move with our fingers to turn the switch on or off is made of plastic, a good insulator. Without insulators, the use of electricity for household purposes would be difficult or nearly impossible.

At the flick of the light switch, the spring-loaded lever extends to the metal contact and completes the circuit.

CHAPTER FOUR

Citywide Circuits—How We Receive Electricity

ELECTRICITY COMES into our homes 24 hours a day to light our lamps and power our appliances. We hardly think about it until something goes wrong and we have to do without electricity for a while. How does all that electricity get generated, and how does it get transmitted to our homes, schools, and workplaces?

All electricity is produced from other forms of energy. For example, a hydroelectric plant uses the energy of rushing water to generate electricity. Most power plants burn fossil fuels—coal, oil, or natural gas. The energy released by the burning fuel turns water into steam, and that steam is harnessed to make electricity. A nuclear power plant uses the energy released by atoms of uranium to heat water into steam.

Electricity can be generated through wind power harnessed by wind turbines.

Whether a power plant uses rushing water or steam, the next steps are the same. The water or steam spins the blades of large machines called turbines. The turbines are connected to

Because excessive heat can result from generating electricity, many power plants need cooling towers that release the heat by evaporating water into the atmosphere.

THE POWER CYCLE

Generation

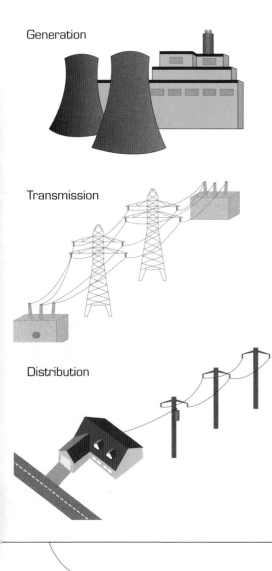

Transmission

Distribution

Generators within a power plant produce a current with a voltage of more than 20,000 volts. The current is sent to a large device outside the plant called a step-up transformer, which increases the voltage to as much as 765,000 volts so the current can be transmitted over a long distance.

An electric current is carried away from the power plant by large transmission lines—heavy cables strung between tall towers. The transmission lines carry the current to places called substations. There, step-down transformers decrease the voltage to as low as 2,000 volts.

Some of this medium-voltage current is then transmitted directly to factories and other large consumers of power. The rest is further reduced to 120 volts and supplied to homes, offices, and stores. Because all electric current must move in a closed circuit, a second set of transmission lines carries the current back to the power station. The path is then complete, and the power cycle continues.

other large machines called generators, which produce either AC or DC current. The first large electrical generators, constructed in the late 1800s, produced DC current. But all the generators in modern power plants are AC generators.

Transmission lines are needed to transmit the current over long distances.

The Blackout of 2003

On a hot day in August 2003, about 50 million Americans and Canadians suddenly lost their electricity. In New York City, many people were stranded on underground trains that run on

Without electricity providing air conditioning to many homes and businesses in New York City during the 2003 blackout, people took refuge outside in the cool night air.

electricity. Airports in New York, New Jersey, Ohio, and elsewhere canceled flights. People in many areas suffered from the heat because their air conditioners were useless.

This power loss, called a blackout, affected much of the northeastern United States and south-central Canada. Investigators learned that the blackout began in Ohio. Three transmission lines that were sagging in the heat touched the tops of trees. That contact caused electricity in the lines to flow through the trees to the ground. The disrupted current from those three lines caused disruptions elsewhere.

Computer systems were supposed to prevent the problem from spreading, but they failed. Ohio was soon short of electricity. The state began drawing large amounts of electricity from other areas through a power grid—a huge network of connected power plants and transmission lines. Automatic systems in several states stopped the sudden flow of electricity to Ohio. The automated systems also shut down 256 power plants.

Besides making people's lives difficult, the blackout showed that the U.S. power grid was less secure than it should be. Experts hoped that improvements to the grid would make future blackouts less likely.

CHAPTER FIVE

Household Circuits

IT'S HARD TO IMAGINE our homes without electricity. Without electricity, we would have no televisions, refrigerators, or air conditioners. We would be without telephones, e-mail, and video games. Modern life and electricity go hand in hand.

Electricity is supplied to our homes for lighting and appliances after a nearby step-down transformer decreases the voltage to 120 volts. Household lights and small appliances are designed to operate at that voltage. Larger appliances, such as electric stoves and clothes dryers, need 240 volts. Since the voltage is only 120 volts, two 120-volt wires are used instead.

All household wiring is parallel, so lights and appliances can be used independently of other devices. All the devices on a 120-volt circuit operate at 120 volts, but their current needs can vary. The

A kitchen can run many appliances at different times because it uses parallel wiring.

> **DID YOU KNOW?**
>
> Model electric trains operate at 12 volts. Because household current is at 120 volts, the operator of a train set must step down the voltage with a small transformer.

current automatically increases or decreases to meet the needs of the lights and appliances that are switched on.

AVOIDING CURRENT OVERLOADS

A household circuit is designed to limit the amount of current in the wires. If a circuit carries too much current, it can get overheated. The heat can melt the insulation around the wires and cause a fire.

Small devices called fuses are designed to shut down an overloaded circuit. A fuse contains a metal strip that melts if the current gets too high, stopping the current's flow. The fuse must then be replaced.

Circuit breakers are also used to shut down an overloaded circuit. There are several kinds of circuit breakers, but the most common contains a metal strip that bends when the current gets too high. This opens the circuit and stops the flow of electricity. All circuit breakers can be reset by hand; they do not have to be replaced. All newer homes are equipped with circuit breakers.

Electrical Fires

Every year, electrical fires occur in nearly 70,000 American homes. Approximately 485 people die in such fires each year. Another 2,300 are injured.

Most electrical fires result from old or faulty wiring, which causes a short circuit. In a short circuit, the current finds a shorter path to follow. This path almost always has less resistance than the path through a light or appliance. With lower resistance, the current surges to dangerous levels, and a fire may result.

To avoid a short circuit, the wiring in older houses and apartments should be checked by an expert, who will decide whether an upgrade is needed. Other fires result

Old or faulty wiring can catch fire from a short circuit.

from overloading household circuits with too many appliances. This, too, causes current to increase to unsafe levels.

Fuses and circuit breakers normally shut off the current in a circuit when it gets too high. Fuses and circuit breakers give a warning that you are using too much current on a circuit. Simply replacing a fuse or resetting a circuit breaker will not solve the problem. It is necessary to reduce the amount of electricity being used on the circuit. If the problem is a short circuit, it is important to find the cause.

The U.S. Fire Administration has a list of do's and don'ts that can help people prevent electrical fires. Some of the most important things to remember are: (1) check wiring often for worn or frayed wires; (2) don't use too many extension cords; and (3) keep easily ignited materials at least 3 feet (1 meter) away from space heaters, irons, and hair dryers.

If an electrical fire occurs in your home, do not throw water on it. It could cause you to be severely shocked. First, have an adult unplug the appliance that caused the fire, if it can be unplugged safely. Then, if you own a class-C fire extinguisher, use it to put out the fire. A class-C extinguisher is designed especially for electrical fires. If you don't have a class-C extinguisher, and the fire is still small, douse the fire with baking soda. If the fire is too big, quickly call the fire department and get out of the house.

PREVENTING SHOCKS

Electric circuits are also designed to prevent electric shocks. Each circuit has a grounding wire that is usually connected to a metal rod in the ground. Appliances are made so that if the electricity could cause damage, the current is sent harmlessly down a special wire in the appliance's power cord. That wire leads to a wall plug that connects to the grounding wire.

Three-prong plugs provide excellent protection against electric shocks because the third prong connects to a grounding wire.

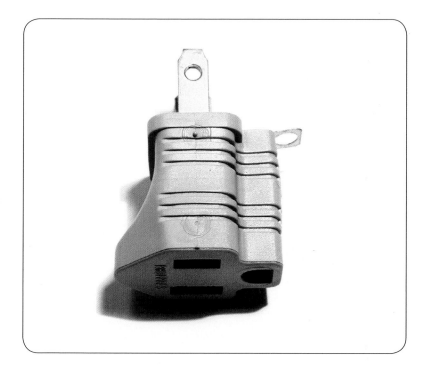

Another type of safety plug is called a polarized plug. These plugs have just two prongs, with one prong wider than the other. The wall socket is designed so that the plug can only be inserted in the proper way. The narrower prong connects to the "hot" wire—the one supplying current. The wider prong connects to the ground wire. Most modern wall sockets accept either a three-prong plug or a polarized plug.

Electricity makes our lives easier and more enjoyable, but it is a powerful force. By using electricity carefully, we can

Appliances with three-prong plugs can be used with an outlet with only two slots, but a small two-pronged device called an adapter is needed.

enjoy its benefits while avoiding its dangers.

From keeping our refrigerators cool to powering our computers, we use electricity every day. When a power outage or
a circuit failure stops the flow of electricity, people often fret
until the current has been restored. In today's world, it is hard
to imagine life without electricity.

Large transformers at a power plant are used to step up the voltage
of an AC current so the current can be transmitted a long distance.

alternating current—current that switches direction many times a second

anion (pronounced AN-ion)—negatively charged ion

cation (pronounced CAT-ion)—positively charged ion

conductor—material through which electric charges move easily; most conductors are metals

direct current—current that always moves in the same direction

electric charge—basic property of matter, carried by electrons and protons

electric circuit—path followed by a flow of charges; for charges to flow, a circuit must be closed, or have no gaps

electric current—flow of electric charges; in most cases, the charges are electrons

insulator—material, such as rubber or plastic, that does not carry an electric current

parallel circuit—circuit in which current follows two or more side-by-side paths

resistance—opposition to the flow of electric charges; a thin wire has more resistance than a thicker wire

series circuit—circuit in which current follows a single path; devices powered by the current are wired in a line, or series

transformer—device that increases or decreases the voltage of an electric current

▸ About 100 lightning bolts strike the earth every second. Each one carries billions and billions of electrons down to the ground. About 100 people in the United States die from lightning strikes each year.

▸ High voltage is usually very dangerous, but not always. A device called a Van de Graaff generator produces extremely high voltages but almost no current. Without a current, a large voltage poses little danger. A classroom version of a Van de Graaff generator produces a voltage difference of as much as 500,000 volts between its domed top and its base. It does this by pulling electrons away from atoms in the dome, causing it to become positively charged. The dome will draw sparks from a hand-held wand and can produce other dramatic electrical effects.

▸ The volt is named for Alessandro Volta, an Italian researcher who lived in the late 1700s and early 1800s. Volta invented the electric battery.

▸ Some animals can produce electric discharges. The best known is the electric eel, which is actually a type of fish. This animal, which lives in rivers of South America, generates electric charges with special cells called electroplates. It can produce a voltage difference across its body of up to 650 volts. When the eel touches prey, its body releases a surge of electric current that stuns or kills the other animal.

When threatened, an electric eel can produce intermittent electric charges for over an hour.

At the Library

Aldrich, Lisa. *Nikola Tesla and the Taming of Electricity.*
  Greensboro, N.C.: Morgan Reynolds Pub., 2005.
Carlson, Laurie. *Thomas Edison for Kids: His Life and Ideas:
  21 Activities.* Chicago: Chicago Review Press, 2006.
Parker, Steve. *The Science of Electricity and Magnetism:
  Projects and Experiments with Electrons and Magnets.*
  Chicago: Heinemann Library, 2005.
Riley, Peter. *Electricity and Power.* North Mankato, Minn.:
  Smart Apple Media, 2006.

On the Web

For more information on this topic, use FactHound.
  1. Go to *www.facthound.com*
  2. Type in this book ID: **0756532671**
  3. Click on the *Fetch It* button.
FactHound will find the best Web sites for you.

On the Road

The Exploratorium
   3601 Lyon St.
   San Francisco, CA 94123
   415/397-5673

The New Detroit Science Center
   5020 John R St.
   Detroit, MI 48202
   313/577-8400

Explore all the Physical Science books

Atoms & Molecules: Building Blocks of the Universe

Chemical Change: From Fireworks to Rust

Electrical Circuits: Harnessing Electricity

Force and Motion: Laws of Movement

Kinetic Energy: The Energy of Motion

Manipulating Light: Reflection, Refraction, and Absorption

The Periodic Table: Mapping the Elements

Physical Change: Reshaping Matter

Waves: Energy on the Move

A complete list of Exploring Science titles is available on our Web site: *www.compasspointbooks.com*